stink outside the box

Other books by Jeremy Greenberg

Sorry I Peed on You
Sorry I Pooped in Your Shoe
Sorry I Barfed in Your Bed
Kitty Hearts Doggy

stink outside the box

the box

Life Advice from Kitty

Jeremy Greenberg

Andrews McMeel
Publishing

Kansas City • Sydney • London

Photographer Credits

Amanda Andrews, Ginger and Lonely Boy, page 61; Sarah Barker, Holly, page 33; Gina DeRenzis, Cuty Patooty, page 22; Alex Dumitrescu, Terry, page 10; Anne M. Fearon-Wood, Frankie, page 34, and Cruiser, page 46; Michael Fox, Pepper, page 6; Carolyn Ganus, Hobbes, page 58; Dorothy E. Harris, Grimalkin and Musetta, page 30; Alice Wong Sau Hing, Kraken and Kraken Jr., page 25; Travis Hunt, Bam Bam, page 26; Julian Hutchings, Scat, page 18; Emmanuel Keller, Tyler, page 45; Heather Klebs, Benny, page 53; Tony Langford, Toby, page 38; Erin Longstreet, Anko, page 50; Bill Marrs, Sweetie, page 29; Lori Morris, Sixtoes, page 37; Esther Muller, Flea, page 57; Ariskina Oksana, Simon, page 13; Niklas Pivic, Blixa, page 42; Claude Paine, Taboo, page 54; Leta Paine, Tippy, page 41; Jodi Payne, Tasha, page 62; Dawn Marie Rappa, Versace, page 14; Alan Rigby, Yoda, page 21; Kathy Slovachek, Natasha, page 9; Renee Tellez, BoBo, page 17; Shauna Vaillancourt, Rocky, page 49.

For my sons, Ben and Seth.

May you always sleep in the sunny spot.

Trying to claw your way to the top will just leave your life in tatters.

KITTY COUNSELOR
Pepper

MOMENT IN PURRSPECTIVE: Knowing that my human will never understand how long her 40-hour work weeks are in cat years and what it's doing to our relationship.

PEPPER SAYS: If I could impart one piece of advice to all young kitties beginning their careers as housecats, it's that you should work smarter and not harder. I remember when I was a young kitten, barely old enough to grow a hairball. No matter how many times I'd shred the toilet paper into a lifeless pile of two-ply fluff, the next morning I'd wake up and the roll wouldn't even have so much as a scratch. It's like someone cleaned up all my work and put a fresh roll out while I was asleep. All of my diligence and hard work was wasted!

It made me begin to question why I was working so hard to destroy toilet paper. It wasn't making any lasting changes. The world wasn't becoming a fluffier place. Now, I stick to projects that make a difference, like chewing on my human's bikini straps. When those unexpectedly unravel at the beach, it's a memory that lasts a lifetime. 🐾

Getting your life in order takes nothing more than a few simple steps.

KITTY COUNSELOR
Natasha

MOMENT IN PURRSPECTIVE: That although my humans have been vaccinated, there are people in less developed music cliques who still suffer from cat scratch fever.

NATASHA SAYS: I know I seem like quite the cool and collected cat, with my vet bills organized neatly right behind my receipts for medical catnip. But I was once such a cluttered wreck that the only decent place I could find to sit was on my human's computer while he was trying to do his taxes. I had to get my 9 lives in order.

I began by organizing all my toys and tin foil balls into a single dusty clump under the couch. Next, I cleaned off any countertops that happened to be littered with pens, pencils, glasses of water, vases, iPads, urns, rare fossils, or any expensive and easily breakable object that had no place on a sleeping surface. And finally, I decided that instead of scattering my poop in a feng shui–like fashion around the house, I'd keep it all in a box in the garage. I must admit, it's really nice finally knowing where all my crap is.

Brains aren't everything.

KITTY COUNSELOR
Terry

MOMENT IN PURRSPECTIVE: Realizing that you can sit on a flat screen TV for warmth. You just have to knock it down first.

TERRY SAYS: Most cats are born knowing how to hunt mice. But I've never caught one. So what? You can't tell everything about a cat by his standardized pest scores. My mommy used to meow to me that I wasn't the sharpest claw on the paw, just because I tried to suckle by biting her ear. And I once fell into the water dish.

But one thing I know is that I am full of grit, and not just because I was rolling around in the loose flower bed soil. I'm not afraid to seek warmth and comfort in places smarter cats wouldn't dare stick their wet noses. Is it dangerous sleeping in a dryer? Yes. But do you know what's more dangerous? Looking back on your life and regretting those moments in which you could've been cozier. 🐾

Don't be surprised by what it will take to get to the top.

KITTY COUNSELOR
Simon

MOMENT IN PURRSPECTIVE: Realizing that despite the name, "catsup" won't help me climb anything.

SIMON SAYS: There will be many positive humans who will support your goal of always being on the highest place. But there also will be bitter, salty to the lick, underachieving humans who try to keep you from climbing as high as you can and some squirrels your ambition will just annoy. My human yells at me every time I jump from the bed to the top of the dresser, for no good reason other than I often crash into her perfume bottles and make her room smell like a brothel for a month.

But I don't let that keep me down. When she puts me outside, I immediately scale a drainpipe to the roof of the house. I always get stuck, and my human has to pop out the window in the upstairs bedroom to get me. But that's fine. It just reminds me that in a cat's life the people you meet on the way up are the same ones you'll meet on the way down. 🐾

Don't drive angry.

MOMENT IN PURRSPECTIVE: Learning that Cat Woman was just a human in a costume and that I'd have to find someone else to have my kittens.

VERSACE SAYS: Every morning when I set down my kitty coffee to get into my kitty car and drive to kitty work, I try to remember that although I'm a professional race-through-the-house kitty, and I am known to sprint from one end of the room to the other, I still should never get behind the paws if I've recently become agitated.

If I've been licked by the dog, I know not to drive. If the human pushes me off the couch while I was deep into a dream about sleeping on the couch, angrily sprinting isn't the answer. Despite the instinct to run, I must casually strut to a new slumber spot. As cats, we will always feel tempted to tear through the house when angry. But the chances of sliding across the floor and bonking your head on the leg of the kitchen table make the risk just not worth it.

Life doesn't end after kittens.

BoBo

MOMENT IN PURRSPECTIVE: Realizing that my human was leaving her shoelaces untied as a subtle hint I needed to get more exercise.

BOBO SAYS: All it takes is one open sliding glass door and one feral alley cat calling your name for your life to change forever. When I had kittens, I was barely a cat myself. My humans found my feral kitty baby-mama and adopted her. Now she just sleeps all day and asks when I'm going to catch her a mouse. The kids have grown up and left the cardboard box. And my humans won't let me outside because of what I got my kitty-mama for our anniversary. I tried to explain that bird guts are customary for the third year.

Back to the point, I thought my life was over. But then I realized that now I could pretty much just sit on the couch all day, sleeping and watching Animal Planet. That's what I wanted to do with my life all along! Never stop searching for your dreams, cats. You'll fall asleep and find them. 🐾

Occasionally things that seem a bit fishy are a bit fishy.

Scat

MOMENT IN PURRSPECTIVE: I don't need "brain food." I just eat it to set a good example for my human.

SCAT SAYS: In a cat's life, there will be times when he will just have to trust his instincts. I know this thing doesn't look like a fish. Fish, as every cat knows, is a bunch of brown, goop-covered chunks that come in a can your human taps with a can opener to taunt you. But it smells and tastes like a fish, so I think I'll eat it anyway. I trust my kitty instincts.

Occasionally I'll be given something that looks like a mouse. It's got a little tail and is fuzzy, but it smells like a piece of felt. What do I do? I trust my instincts and brutally kill it. And let's not forget when I see some wiggling bumps under the cover where my human's toes are. But are they toes or some little bug that needs to be bopped with a paw? I know they're toes—but I still do the right thing and give 'em a bop anyway. Always trust the little voice in your kitty head. You can't let your human's toes think they run the joint. 🐾

Love is truly blind.

Yoda

MOMENT IN PURRSPECTIVE: You can have all the delicious wet food in the world, but if it isn't served by a human who loves you, it might as well be an orange.

YODA SAYS: When I was a young cat, I only rubbed against humans who had nice legs. I figured, "I'm beautiful, I should be with a beautiful human." But those relationships never lasted. They were all just pat, scat, thank-you cat. Then I met my current human.

I wasn't immediately taken by his appearance. When he took off his clothes, he was covered head to toe and front to back in a mat of furry hair—like some animal. I was worried that if I licked him I'd get hairballs. But the human was so into me, all he'd do was sit on the couch and provide me a warm lap. If I'd been superficial, I'd have missed meeting my personal beanbag. Besides, we all look the same with the lights off—although cats unfortunately have excellent night vision. 🐾

The only real prison is in your mind.

KITTY COUNSELOR
Cuty Patooty

MOMENT IN PURRSPECTIVE: Apparently the vacuum cleaner and I are from rival gangs, because whenever he's transported through the house, I'm put in solitary confinement.

CUTY PATOOTY SAYS: Yes, I am an angry kitty. But it's only because I'm in here for a crime I didn't commit. You see, there was this "other cat" (not sure of its color) who snuck into my litter box in the middle of night. He's the one who had runny stool, not me. But here I am, about to go somewhere called "the vet"—which I assume is some maximum security facility for diarrheal offenders. But after spending as much time behind bars as I have (about 5 minutes so far), I can tell you that this is actually the freest I've ever been.

It wasn't until being locked up that I realized our entire feline existence is just one big cage. Think of the cat who asks to go outside, then immediately wants to come back in, then once in promptly begs to return outside. That poor puss is in a cage of his own indecision. I, however, am liberated by accepting my fate. And I really hope the vet has something to cure that "other cat's" diarrhea as well. 🐾

Learn from those
who have come before you.

KITTY COUNSELOR
Kraken Jr.
(featuring Kraken Sr.)

MOMENT IN PURRSPECTIVE: When you finally realize the story that baby kitties are delivered by a stork can't be true—because what bird would create more cats?

KRAKEN JR. SAYS: When I first started being a cat, I have to admit that I didn't respect my elder fuzzballs. I wouldn't listen when they'd howl at me, and I'd bat them in their heads while they slept. But then I realized that the reason they slept all day is because they'd already figured out how to open a screen door with their claws. They knew you didn't have to go all the way to your water dish for a drink if you happened to be in the bathroom.

If I'd only opened my eyes sooner (like when I was 8–14 days old), I would've realized that the older cats weren't just there to push me down the stairs for their own amusement. They were there to teach. Now when an old cat misses the cat box, I don't laugh. I take notes.

This is where I hide
when my human is half in the bag.

KITTY COUNSELOR:
Bam Bam

MOMENT IN PURRSPECTIVE: Some days I just feel like I'm invisible to the world. But for the days I don't, I'm thankful I have this bag to hide in.

BAM BAM SAYS: Occasionally, some humans will drink too much of a really yucky liquid that makes them laugh and stick sunglasses on cats, no matter how many times we meow that we don't need sunglasses because we have an extra set of eyelids. And some humans will blow a weird smoke in our faces that makes us crave Doritos and makes our whiskers feel, like, totally amazing.

When there's a human in your life like this, just remember that they are not as suave as cats. If they didn't have this liquid or funny smoke, they would find it harder to mate or muster up the courage to talk to someone with whom they'd enjoy mating. Treat your human like the dog when they're in this state: Hide from him until he falls asleep on the floor.

Unfamiliar problems will always seem quite hairy at first.

MOMENT IN PURRSPECTIVE: Learning that a cat's body is 80 percent water and finally understanding why I'm always angry.

SWEETIE SAYS: It's a cat fact of life that you will occasionally have to win a howling contest against your arch enemy, the mirror cat (and you know he's your arch enemy because he arches his back). Humans use mirrors to make sure their clothes are covered in our fur before going outside. Also lurking in these mirrors is a cat every bit as hissy and as fluffy as you are (and admittedly quite handsome).

This cat will leave you alone, but first you must adorably howl and swat at it so it knows you're not afraid of appearing silly in front of your human. Once you prove that you're no scaredy cat, he'll ignore you if you ignore him. With all the real fights you'll have with lids of milk jugs or a dog's wagging tail, there's just no place for cat-on-reflection violence.

Find someone you can grow incontinent with.

KITTY COUNSELOR
Grimalkin
(featuring Mrs. Musetta the Calico)

MOMENT IN PURRSPECTIVE: Just because your partner shuts her eyes, it doesn't mean she isn't thinking about you.

GRIMALKIN SAYS: As in love as we are, my relationship to Musetta isn't all snuggles and butt licks. Lately, she's been getting very sensitive when I watch her eat, even throwing total hissy fits if I suggest she maybe not clean out her bowl in a single sitting. I'm just concerned for her health, but she says her increased appetite is due to menopaws. Also, when I get bored I chase her around the house until she vomits. And when she's stuck outside and meowing at me through the window, I'll pretend I don't see her.

But I'll tell you one place where Musetta can never be left outside: my heart. Deep down, there is not another feline I'd rather antagonize. She's the one. Just remember that long-term relationships aren't always easy. But as soon as you accept that you'll never meet a better cat, you can have quite a happy life. 🐾

Travel to far-off and distant bags.

KITTY COUNSELOR
Holly

MOMENT IN PURRSPECTIVE: Climbing around in my human's personal documents box and learning I was adopted. I guess my last name used to be "Shelter."

HOLLY SAYS: This is a big world, and no cat should go through her life without visiting as many bags and boxes as she can. And to challenge your comfort zone, try to fit in a box that's too small. Also see if you can fit in the child human's backpack; you might find a salty potato chip at the bottom. And by all means, don't go through life without sitting in both colors of the laundry basket. How else will you know if the socks in the light green one are just as comfortable as the warm towels in the blue one?

It's not true that curiosity killed the cat. That's just a rumor spread by other cats who don't want you to know what's inside the unraveled sleeping bag in the closet. 🐾

Just because life can be disappointing, it doesn't mean you have to be disappointed.

KITTY COUNSELOR
Frankie

MOMENT IN PURRSPECTIVE: When my human tried to get me registered as a therapy cat, but all I qualified for was shock therapy.

FRANKIE SAYS: There are moments in life that will just leave you scratching your head, or probably bugging your human to do so. You'll come in the house after having hung out with a skunk, and for no reason you'll be plopped into a tub of tomato juice. A dog you thought was your friend will suddenly try to fit your head in its mouth, just because you were feeling kneady and started giving him a massage. Or you'll be asleep, and a dumb teenager human will pop a bag above your head.

Life isn't always a bowl of crunchies. But you don't have to sleep on the top corner of the bookcase for a week. If you learn to accept that a cat is doomed to be perfect in an imperfect world, you won't get as upset when someone calls your close relationship with the dog just a case of kennel fever and remarks that cat–dog relationships rarely last. 🐾

An extra toe is nothing to worry about.

Sixtoes

MOMENT IN PURRSPECTIVE: That there's probably a deep psychological reason why I enjoy chewing the fingers out of gloves.

SIXTOES SAYS: When I used to get teased about having extra toes, I'd get so angry that I'd want to flip the bird, but because of my extra digits I could never figure out how. My humans used to show me off at dinner parties and say, "Look at our mutant cat!" Mutant? I was so distraught that I considered jumping off a bridge. But I'd have to do it 9 times, and that was just too much work.

I decided I had no choice but to embrace my plus-size paws. I couldn't spend my entire life hoping to be adopted by a cat lady with a foot fetish. I just had to accept that some people will make fun of what they can't understand and will become jealous that they don't have extra toes to more quickly bury their poops. 🐾

Ever have one of those lives when you just can't face the day?

KITTY COUNSELOR
Toby

MOMENT IN PURRSPECTIVE: That my depression had nothing to do with my human leaving for work every day. It had to do with her returning.

TOBY SAYS: Do you find it hard to get up in the mornings? Do you find yourself just wanting to sleep all day but then are up all night and so full of energy that you can't help but run around the house waking everyone up? Are you occasionally delusional enough to think you can bury food you don't like in solid kitchen-floor surfaces? Do you ever self-medicate by eating grass? Are there days when you just want to be completely left alone?

Well, good news, you're a perfectly healthy cat! And if you notice that your human has suddenly stopped getting out of bed, you should go cuddle with her. She'll need your support as she deals with being a healthy cat—which is essentially the same thing as a clinically depressed human.

Love your enemies, even if they can be real snakes in the grass.

KITTY COUNSELOR
Tippy

MOMENT IN PURRSPECTIVE: Seeing a bird fly into a window, which started the dog barking, waking the baby and making the human throw the dog outside—at which time I snuck out and found the bird—as well as the realization that everything in life truly does happen for a reason.

TIPPY SAYS: If you meet someone or something with whom you do not see eye to eye, or scale to whisker, try to think about what you two have in common. Let's say you happen upon a real snake in the grass. Just remember that you actually aren't that different. You both love mice. You both hate having your tails stepped on, and you both are known to hiss. Not to mention, you both love sunning yourselves. If we focus on what we have in common with our enemies, it will help us forget how delicious they are.

Accept that some cats can eat whatever they want and still look great.

KITTY COUNSELOR
Blixa

MOMENT IN PURRSPECTIVE: Becoming so comfortable with my body that I didn't mind walking in front of the window naked.

BLIXA SAYS: It used to be that a cat was appreciated for her ability to catch barn mice and for the warmth she could generate while sleeping on a sick grandparent. But now humans have created this thing called the Internet, which they use to chronicle the lives of cats, as well as store videos of human dads being hit by baseballs in their castratables. Humans think it's hilarious when a cat is so fat she gets stuck in cat doors and will share movies of frumpy, flummoxed felines sadly plugging up a hole in the door to the garage.

But no matter how much I try to become a fat cat, I can't gain a pound. Some cats can just walk by a full food bowl and instantly add a waddling tummy. Their human will say it's just fur, but they're being modest. Most cats have to accept that the ability to get that fat is just something you're born with. It's one of those very special genetic gifts, like being furless and hypoallergenic. You just have to be chosen.

Who are you calling a pussy cat?

KITTY COUNSELOR
Tyler

MOMENT IN PURRSPECTIVE: The day I realized I was the toughest cat alive was when my humans took me in to be castrated and the knife kept breaking.

TYLER SAYS: Let me tell you kitties what toughness really is: Toughness is the ability to sleep in the sunny spot, even if you start to get a bit too hot. Toughness is climbing right back onto your human's lap after she mistakenly says, "Go away, kitty" and throws you off. Toughness is knowing when to howl at the neighbor cat through the bay window. Does he think he can just walk along my fence without facing the consequences of an arched back and fluffed tail? My cat family has been in this neighborhood for 7 generations, which is about 15 months.

And my human could never say I wasn't tough. Whenever she tries to take me to the vet, she learns that I am a professional cage fighter. Don't let anyone ever call you a 'fraidy cat. The only thing kitties are truly scared of is a grandpa human's wheelchair. 🐾

Don't be such a baby.

KITTY COUNSELOR
Cruiser

MOMENT IN PURRSPECTIVE: Hearing gangsta rap for the first time and realizing that there are others who have suffered the way I have.

CRUISER SAYS: In life, you have to be a big cute kitty. Don't just sit there helplessly, hoping a human will notice that you're cold. Pull yourself up by your own puss-and-boot straps and meow pathetically until the human swaddles you in a baby blanket. Be a take-charge kind of kitten.

Later on in life you might be hungry and won't want to wait until the human feeds you. It's best you start learning to fend for yourself, so when that time comes, you simply know to paw open the pantry and knock over the bag of cat kibble. The sound of your well-earned meal scattering across the kitchen floor will probably send the dog and the human sprinting toward you. Others are naturally attracted to cats with a can-do attitude. 🐾

Drink 8 glasses of someone else's water a day.

KITTY COUNSELOR

Rocky

MOMENT IN PURRSPECTIVE: A little-known fact is that ancient Egyptians turned their water into beer to keep cats from drinking all of it.

ROCKY SAYS: Want a quick way to give your fur back the bounce and shine it once had as a kitten? Drink at least 8 glasses of your human's water every day. In addition to having an irresistibly pettable pelt, you'll find that staying hydrated will help a cat maintain a more positive attitude. The dog becomes less annoying, flies on window sills are easier to catch, and you'll even find yourself having a bit more empathy for the poor, dehydrated raccoon who breaks into your house to feast on your Friskies.

So remember, if you drink plenty of your human's water, the glass will always seem half full—though you may have to reach your paw in to get a sip. 🐾

Maintain a low profile.

Anko

MOMENT IN PURRSPECTIVE: The human memory is only about 2 seconds. How else can you explain why mine keeps trying to wake me after I don't respond?

ANKO SAYS: If you really want attention from humans, the best way to get it is by ignoring them. I know this can be hard when you want them to give you a head scratch, or they're sleeping under a warm blanket not yet matted with an un-washable thicket of your fur. But trust me, if you keep your head down and your tail tucked between your legs, your human will want you so bad he'll probably leave catnip on his pillow.

If a human thinks he can get you on his head too easily, he won't be interested. But if you act like your human barely exists, and you don't even care when he pets the dog (it will be hard not to show some jealousy—especially since the dog is such a pet slut), you will find that when you do actually enter the bedroom, the human will beg you to sleep on his head. In fact, he may take a picture of you on his head and post it on Facebook so everyone can see your new relationship status. 🐾

Don't scratch the small stuff (or your butt).

KITTY COUNSELOR
Benny

MOMENT IN PURRSPECTIVE: Noticing that on Halloween humans dress like cats to get candy, but I look like a cat every day and get nothing.

BENNY SAYS: I can't just sit here and tell you that I haven't made mistakes in my life. Clearly, I've let certain things get to me, and it wasn't until a rash of hair-raising incidents that I was finally able to let it go.

What this painful experience has taught me is that in life it never pays to scratch the small stuff. When you do get the itch to scratch, just make a point of sleeping with your human for comfort. Soon, she'll also understand what's eating you, and can get you some beautiful new neckwear. There's nothing like jewelry to help you forget your problems. But if you just bite and bite, your problem can be much worse than whatever was initially bugging you. If you don't want to go to the vet (and no cat wants to admit they need professional help), remember, don't scratch the small stuff—or your butt.

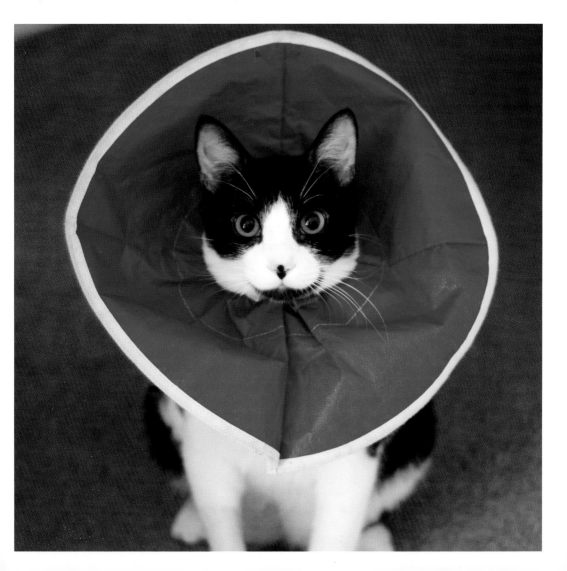

You are more than your emotions.

Taboo

MOMENT IN PURRSPECTIVE: If your human yells at you for waking her in the middle of an excellent dream and throws you out of the bedroom, it's not your fault. You're just too real for her.

TABOO SAYS: Sometimes cats will get so angry that we'll swat at anything that moves. It doesn't even have to be real. We'll take our aggression out on shadows, lasers, and even our human's pony tail, though it's done nothing to us other than mimic the scurry of fleeing prey. Other times, we'll feel disconnected and aloof, looking down on humans from atop the china hutch, completely immune to their charms and feather toys. And still there are other moments in which a kitty will feel playful, mischievous, or sad.

So which of these is it? Who are we really? The answer is that we are more than how we feel at any one time. You just can't put us in any one box. Eventually, we'll climb into all of them. 🐾

Having unique facial hair will definitely make you seem more hip.

KITTY COUNSELOR

Flea

MOMENT IN PURRSPECTIVE: Rolling your own toilet paper may look cool, but it shreds way too fast.

FLEA SAYS: Many young kittens see my hepcat mustache and ask if they could ever be as much of a cool cat as Flea. My relaxed, nonchalant meow is that, yes, they could be. Even if they aren't blessed with a perfect furry wisp of white mustache fur, if a kitty has the latest scratching post, he can be a cool cat. If you sleep on the right books and eat only locally sourced kibble, your awesomeness will be equal to that of my mustache.

But the real question is, why would you want to appear trendy? It's okay to enjoy the fashions of the day, but eventually you need to learn that it's all just fur deep. Sure, I have an amazing mustache. But I'd still be amazing without it—just maybe not as cute. 🐾

Embrace changes
to your environment.

KITTY COUNSELOR
Hobbes

MOMENT IN PURRSPECTIVE: Seeing Morris the Cat NOT eating 9 Lives and wondering what else from my kittenhood was a lie.

HOBBES SAYS: It is a common misconception that cats are resistant to change. Look at me, for example. My human moved my favorite outside chair, the one that gives me a bird's eye view of the birdies and the ability to scope for approaching pooches. A younger kitten might've gotten his tail all twitchy. But I simply adapted by refusing to move even as my human lifted the chair and hung it on the railing.

Was I a bit nervous when the chair started to tip? Yes. Did I get annoyed when my human gently shook the chair and said, "Get off, Hobbes"? I did. But dealing with change means that you sometimes dig your claws in and refuse to move. You didn't pee on the chair legs for nothing. 🐾

Learn to forgive your siblings for what they did to you as a kitten.

KITTY COUNSELOR
Ginger
(featuring Lonely Boy)

MOMENT IN PURRSPECTIVE: Realizing the rock band Nine Inch Nails didn't sing songs about being declawed.

GINGER SAYS: Even the most well-adjusted cats can tell stories about how their siblings bit or scratched them, barged in on them while they were using the cat box, or otherwise made their kittenhood so tough that it's amazing they all didn't rebel by becoming Goth kittens (which would've been easy for my brother because of his black fur). But no matter how harried your siblings may have made you, to fully become the cat your mother intended you to be when she met your feral father in a dumpster, you have to accept that what we do as kittens doesn't have to control who we are as cats.

I know many cats who are bitten want to bite. But you can be a nice kitty-kitty, even if your siblings would jump off tables and bat you in the head. They had just as much trouble as you did and would love to call to apologize if only their paws weren't too big to use a phone.

Brown nosing will always make you seem fake.

KITTY COUNSELOR
Tasha

MOMENT IN PURRSPECTIVE: It isn't until you run out of catnip that you learn who your real friends are.

TASHA SAYS: One thing all cats learn sooner or later is that you can't just go around complimenting other cats on the smell of their butts or grooming them excessively. Not unless you want a swat across the whiskers. I understand that some cats love to come running when a human makes kissy sounds. But no human will respect you if you try to get your way by giving false meows or purring when you're actually just nervous.

And even if you do trick a human into liking you, will you like yourself? Certainly no cat will respect you. So in all interactions you'll find it easier to be yourself. If you want to scratch someone, they'll just have to accept you for who you are and get a bandage. 🐾

Stink Outside the Box

Andrews McMeel Publishing, LLC
an Andrews McMeel Universal company
1130 Walnut Street, Kansas City, Missouri 64106

www.andrewsmcmeel.com

14 15 16 17 18 TEN 10 9 8 7 6 5 4 3 2 1

ISBN: 978-1-4494-5659-7

Library of Congress Control Number: 2014935731

www.jeremygreenberg.com

ATTENTION: SCHOOLS AND BUSINESSES
Andrews McMeel books are available at quantity discounts with bulk purchase
for educational, business, or sales promotional use. For information,
please e-mail the Andrews McMeel Publishing Special Sales Department:
specialsales@amuniversal.com